KIDS' TRAVEL GUIDE

USA & SAN FRANCISCO

FlyingKids Presents:

Kids' Travel Guide
USA & San Francisco

Author: Kelsey Fox, Shiela H. Leon

Editor: Carma Graber

Designer: Slavisa Zivkovic

Cover design: Francesca Guido

Illustrations: Slavisa Zivkovic, Francesca Guido

Published by FlyingKids

Visit us @ www.theflyingkids.com

Contact us: leonardo@theflyingkids.com

ISBN 978-1499677881

Copyright © 2015 Shira Halperin and FlyingKids

All rights reserved. No part of this publication may be reproduced, stored in retrieval systems, or transmitted by any means, including electronic, mechanical, photocopying, or otherwise, without prior written permission of the publisher and copyright holder.

Although the authors and FlyingKids have taken all reasonable care in preparing this book, we make no warranty about the accuracy or completeness of its content and, to the maximum extent permitted, disclaim all liability arising from its use.

Table of Contents

Dear Parents 4
Hi, Kids! 5
A travel diary—the beginning 6
Preparations at home 8
Let's meet the United States of America 10
The compass rose / Borders 12
About the US states 13
About the US capital—Washington, DC 16
About flags, symbols, and coins 17
Once upon a time: some history 21
About American culture and Americans 27
About American food 35
Trivia—what do you know about the USA? 38
About San Francisco, California 39
Some history: the Gold Rush 43
Things you'll see only in San Francisco 44
Getting around in San Francisco 45
About Union Square 47
Chinatown 49
The Golden Gate Bridge 52
Fisherman's Wharf and Pier 39 54
Exploring Alcatraz 58
North Beach—Little Italy 60
Telegraph Hill and Coit Tower 61
Golden Gate Park 62
Lombard Street 64
Summary of the trip 65
Games and quizzes 66
A journal 70

This is the only page for parents in this book ... 😉

Dear Parents,

If you bought this book, you're probably planning a family trip with your kids. You are spending a lot of time and money in the hopes that this family vacation will be pleasant and fun. Of course, you would like your children to get to know the place you are visiting—a little of its geography, local history, important sites, culture, customs, and more. And you hope they will always remember the trip as a very special experience.

The reality is often quite different. Parents find themselves frustrated as they struggle to convince their kids to join a tour or visit a landmark, while the kids just want to stay in and watch TV. Or the kids are glued to their mobile devices and don't pay much attention to the new sights and places of interest. Many parents are disappointed when they return home and discover that their kids don't remember much about the trip and the new things they learned.

That's exactly why the Kids' Travel Guide series was created.

With the Kids' Travel Guides, young children become researchers and active participants in the trip. During the vacation, kids will read relevant facts about the place you are visiting. The Kids' Travel Guides include puzzles, tasks to complete, useful tips, and other recommendations along the way.

The kids will meet Leonardo—their tour guide. Leonardo encourages them to experiment, explore, and be more involved in the family's activities—as well as to learn new information and make memories throughout the trip. In addition, kids are encouraged to document and write about their experiences during the trip, so that when you return home, they will have a memoir that will be fun to look at and reread again and again.

The Kids' Travel Guides support children as they get ready for the trip, visit new places, learn new things, and finally, return home.

The Kids' Travel Guide — USA & San Francisco focuses on the US and the City by the Bay—San Francisco, California. In it, children will learn about the United States of America—its geography, history, unique culture, traditions, and more—along with background information on San Francisco and its special attractions. The San Francisco portion of the book concentrates on central sites that are recommended for children. At each of these sites, interesting facts, action items, and quizzes await your kids. You, the parents, are invited to participate, or to find an available bench and relax while you enjoy your active children.

Have a great Family Trip!

Hi, kids!

If you are reading this book, it means you are lucky—you are going to San Francisco, California, in the United States of America! You may have noticed that your parents are getting ready for the journey. They have bought travel guides, looked for information on the Internet, and printed pages of information. They are talking to friends and people who have already visited the USA and San Francisco, in order to learn about it and know what to do, where to go, and when … But this is not just another guidebook for your parents.

Leonardo

This book is for you only — the young traveler.

So what is this book all about?

First and foremost, meet Leonardo, your very own personal guide on this trip. Leonardo has visited many places around the world. (Guess how he got there?) He will be with you throughout the book and the trip. Leonardo will tell you all about the places you will visit … It is always good to learn a little about the country and city you are visiting and its history beforehand. Leonardo will give you many ideas, quizzes, tips, and other surprises. He will accompany you while you are packing and leaving home. He will stay in the hotel with you (don't worry—it doesn't cost more money)! And he will see the sights with you until you return home.

A travel diary – the beginning!

Going to San Francisco, USA !!!

How did you get to San Francisco?
By plane ✈ / train 🚆 / car 🚗 / other

Date of arrival _____   Time _____

Date of departure _____

All in all, we will stay in San Francisco for _____ days.

Is this your first visit?   YES   NO

Where will you sleep?
In a hotel / in a campsite / in an apartment / other

What sites are you planning to visit?
_____
_____
_____

What special activities are you planning to do?
_____
_____

Who is traveling?

Write down the names of the family members traveling with you and their answers to the questions.

Paste a picture of your family.

Name: _____
Age: _____
Has he or she visited the USA or San Francisco before? yes / no
WHAT IS THE MOST EXCITING THING ABOUT YOUR UPCOMING TRIP?
_____
_____
_____

Name: _____
Age: _____
Has he or she visited the USA or San Francisco before? yes / no
WHAT IS THE MOST EXCITING THING ABOUT YOUR UPCOMING TRIP?
_____
_____
_____

Name: _____
Age: _____
Has he or she visited the USA or San Francisco before? yes / no
WHAT IS THE MOST EXCITING THING ABOUT YOUR UPCOMING TRIP?
_____
_____
_____

Name: _____
Age: _____
Has he or she visited the USA or San Francisco before? yes / no
WHAT IS THE MOST EXCITING THING ABOUT YOUR UPCOMING TRIP?
_____
_____
_____

Name: _____
Age: _____
Has he or she visited the USA or San Francisco before? yes / no
WHAT IS THE MOST EXCITING THING ABOUT YOUR UPCOMING TRIP?
_____
_____
_____

Preparations at home – do not forget …!

Mom or Dad will take care of packing clothes (how many pairs of pants, which comb to take …). So Leonardo will only tell you about the stuff he thinks you may want to bring along to the USA and San Francisco.

Here's the Packing List Leonardo made for you. You can check off each item as you pack it:

- *Kids' Travel Guide — USA & San Francisco*—of course!
- Comfortable walking shoes
- A raincoat (One that folds up is best—sometimes it rains without warning …)
- A hat (and sunglasses, if you want)
- Pens and pencils
- Crayons and markers (It is always nice to color and paint.)
- A notebook or writing pad (You can use it for games or writing, or to draw or doodle in when you're bored …)
- A book to read
- Your smartphone/tablet or camera
- _____
- _____

Pack your things in a small bag (or **backpack**). You may also want to take these things:

- **Snacks**, *fruit*, *candy*, and *chewing gum*. If you are flying, it can help a lot during takeoff and landing, when there's pressure in your ears.

- Some games you can play while sitting down: *electronic games*, *booklets* of *crossword puzzles*, connect-the-numbers, etc.

Now let's see if you can *find 12 items* you should take on a trip in this *word search puzzle*:

- ☐ Leonardo
- ☐ walking shoes
- ☐ hat
- ☐ raincoat
- ☐ crayons
- ☐ book
- ☐ pencil
- ☐ camera
- ☑ snacks
- ☐ fruit
- ☐ patience
- ☐ good mood

P	A	T	I	E	N	C	E	A	W	F	G
E	L	R	T	S	G	Y	J	W	A	T	O
Q	E	Y	U	Y	K	Z	K	M	L	W	O
H	O	S	N	A	S	N	Y	S	K	G	D
A	N	R	Z	C	P	E	N	C	I	L	M
C	A	M	E	R	A	A	W	G	N	E	O
R	R	A	I	N	C	O	A	T	G	Q	O
Y	D	S	G	I	R	K	Z	K	S	H	D
S	O	A	C	O	A	E	T	K	H	A	T
F	R	U	I	T	Y	Q	O	V	O	D	A
B	O	O	K	F	O	H	Z	K	E	R	T
T	K	Z	K	A	N	S	I	E	S	Y	U
O	V	I	E	S	S	N	A	C	K	S	P

9

Let's meet the United States of America

The United States of America (USA) is a huge and unique country that does almost everything in a big way! It is the third largest country in the world 😮. You can think of the US as more than just a country. In fact, it is a federation* of 50 small countries, called states, that are all united under one main government.

> * Federation: many countries or states united into one group. Each of the countries is independent and governs itself, but they are all part of a bigger government that takes care of the needs and problems they share.

Have you heard of New York City? Orlando? Boston? Las Vegas? What about the Grand Canyon and Disneyland?

Indeed, the United States has amazing attractions of all kinds—from beautiful parks and cities to interesting and surprising landmarks and events, as well as people from all cultures around the world—in short, everything you need to travel, have fun, and find lots of new and fascinating things!

How big is the US?

From the East Coast to the West Coast, it's about 3,000 miles (or nearly 5,000 kilometers). That's a long way!

The US has all kinds of weather too. In the North, winter is very cold with lots of snow.

In the southern states, it stays warmer and hardly ever snows.

The US Southwest is a desert area, and in the Northwest, it's damp and rainy a lot of the time.

What is the weather like in the place you're visiting?

Quizzes!

We've said that the United States is the third largest country in the world. Do you know what the two biggest countries are (*in amount of land*)?

1 _____ 2 _____

ANSWERS: 1 Russia, 2 Canada

This is the world map.

Where is the United States on the map? Can you draw a line around the US?

The compass rose/borders

The compass rose is a drawing that shows the directions: North-South-East-West. North is always at the top of the map, and from that you can know the rest of the directions. When you need to find a place, you can use a compass. The compass shows the compass rose, and the needle always points north. This helps you to navigate and figure out where places are, so you can get from one place to another.

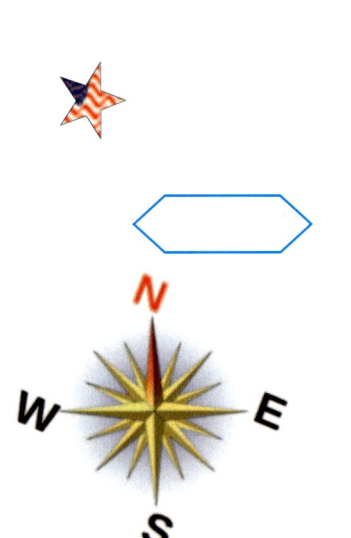

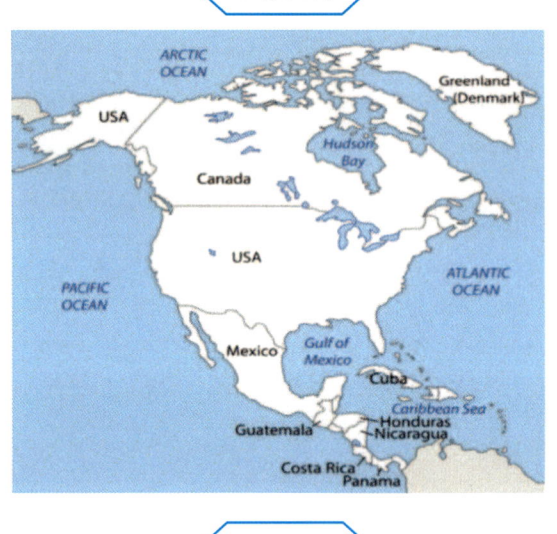

Mark the three missing directions in the blank squares.

Borders

Lines on the map show the borders between countries or states. These lines mark the beginning and end of each country or state's land. When you're traveling, you'll see different kinds of borders: Natural borders are made by rivers, mountains, oceans, etc. When there is no natural border between countries or states, sometimes a fence or a gateway marks the border, and sometimes the border is just shown by a sign.

Look at the map. What forms the borders of the United States?

In the north: _____   In the south: _____

On the east: _____   On the west: _____

About the US states

This is a map of the USA that shows all the states.

Try to find the state that has the most neighboring states. How many other states touch its borders?

Quizzes!

What state has the longest name?

ANSWERS

Actually, there are two states: Missouri and Tennessee are each bordered by eight other states.

ANSWERS

Massachusetts, North Carolina, South Carolina

Did you know?
The state of Alaska is nearer to Russia than to the other US states 😮.

In fact, the states of Alaska and Hawaii aren't connected to the other 48 states at all. Hawaii, in the Pacific Ocean, is the only US state completely made up of islands.

Did you know?
The United States has more than 300 million people 😮!

How many people live in your country? ____

New York City is the biggest US city, and more than **eight million** people live there. The second biggest city is **Los Angeles**, with more than **three million** residents.

Did you know?

In the state of Montana, there are three times as many cows as there are people.

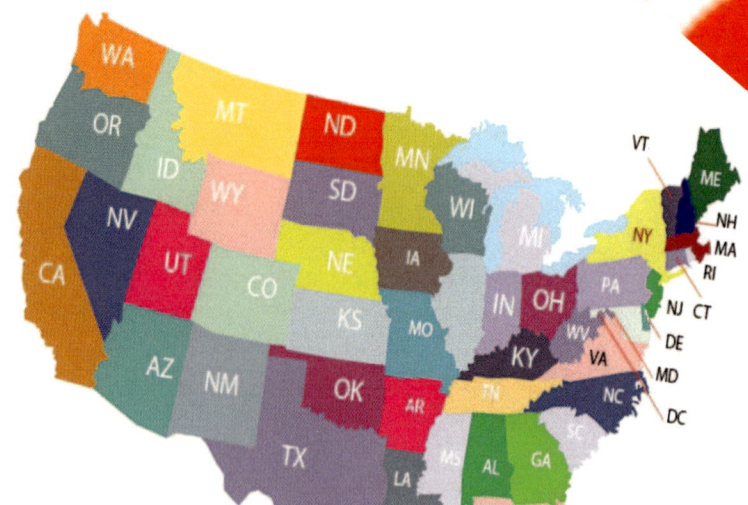

Leonardo looked at a map of the United States, but all the names of the states had been shortened to two letters. Now Leonardo can't figure out the name of each state. Can you help him?

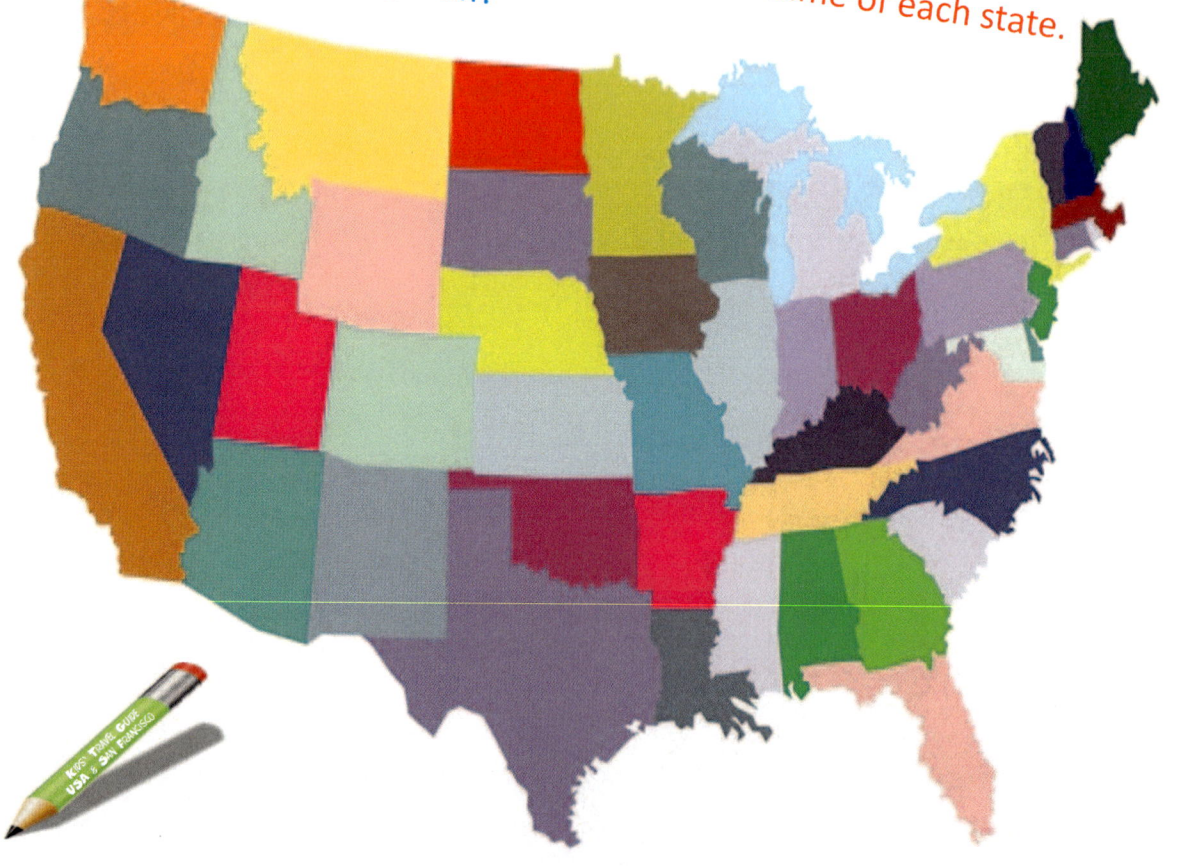

14

Five important facts about the United States got mixed up.
Can you connect each question to the right answer?

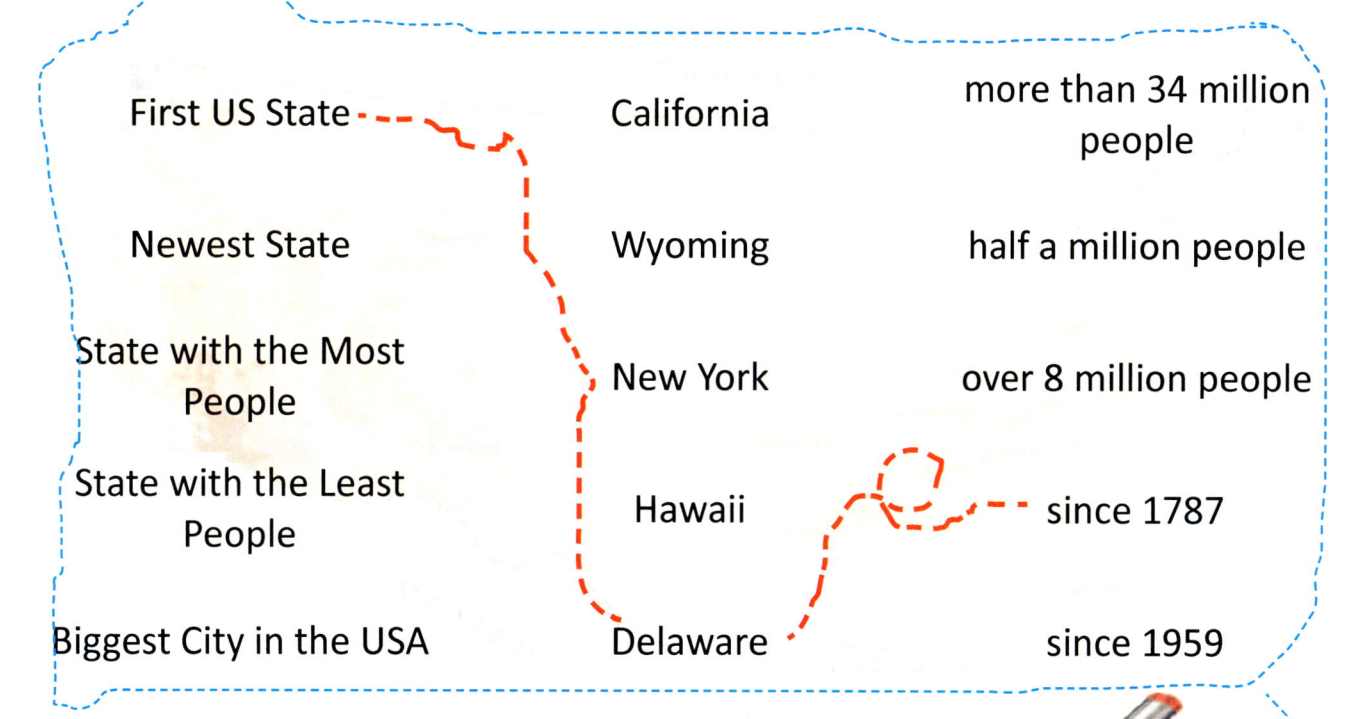

First US State	California	more than 34 million people
Newest State	Wyoming	half a million people
State with the Most People	New York	over 8 million people
State with the Least People	Hawaii	since 1787
Biggest City in the USA	Delaware	since 1959

Did you know?

Alaska's coastline is longer than the coastlines of all the other 49 US states put together.

Quizzes!

What is the capital of the United States?

1. Las Vegas
2. Washington, DC
3. Boston
4. New York

Answer
Washington, DC

Answers:

First US State — Delaware — since 1787
Newest State — Hawaii — since 1959
State with the Most People — California — more than 34 million people
State with the Least People — Wyoming — half a million people
Biggest City in the USA — New York — over 8 million people

About the US capital — Washington, DC

Each of the 50 states in the United States has its own capital. The national capital of all 50 states is Washington, DC. It is named after the first president of the United States, George Washington. The "DC" stands for "District of Columbia." "DC" helps people know you are talking about the capital city and not the state of Washington. Washington, DC, sits on the banks of the Potomac River, next to the states of Virginia and Maryland.

All the most important decisions of the United States are made in Washington, DC. At the center of the city stands the impressive Capitol Building. This is where the Congress meets. Each state sends representatives to Congress, and together they make the US laws and the decisions about relationships with other countries. The leader of the United States is the president. The president and the president's family live in a huge house called the White House, and the president takes care of the problems of the country and sometimes the whole world.

This is the seal of the District of Columbia.

This is the flag of Washington, DC.

Quizzes! Do you recognize the building in the picture? Who lives there?

Answer

This is the White House, where the United States President and first family live—and even their cats and dogs!

About flags, symbols, and coins

This is the United States flag. It has 13 red-and-white stripes and a blue rectangle with 50 stars. The flag was designed in 1777. At that time, the country was made up of 13 colonies that were fighting the Revolutionary War to win their independence from Great Britain. The flag had one stripe and one star for each colony.

After the war, the colonies became the United States, and many more states joined the US over the years. (Read about this in the chapter "Once upon a Time.") The 13 stripes on the flag have always stayed the same—to stand for the original 13 colonies. But a new star was added to the flag every time a new state joined the United States, and the flag now has 50 stars.

This is the United States flag as seen in 1777.

How were the colors for the flag chosen?

Each color has a meaning:

Red stands for hardiness (being strong and sturdy) and valor (bravery).

White stands for purity and innocence.

Blue stands for vigilance (watching out for danger), perseverance (sticking with something even when it's hard), and justice.

The symbol of the United States — the Great Seal

Look at the Seal: In the center, there's an eagle—a symbol for strength, courage, and freedom. The eagle holds 13 arrows in one hand. Do you remember what the number 13 stands for? The 13 original colonies of the United States. In the other hand, the eagle holds an olive branch. The olive branch is a symbol of peace, and the arrows stand for war. You can see that the eagle is looking toward the olive branch—and this shows that the US wants peace more than war.

The eagle is holding a saying written in Latin. It means "Out of Many, One"—one nation created from 13 colonies and the people of many races, religions, and countries. Above the eagle, there's a white cloud around golden rays and a blue sky with 13 stars. A shield with 13 red-and-white stripes covers the eagle's chest.

The Great Seal is put on foreign treaties and other papers signed by the US President.

Did you know?

The bald eagle is the national bird of the United States.

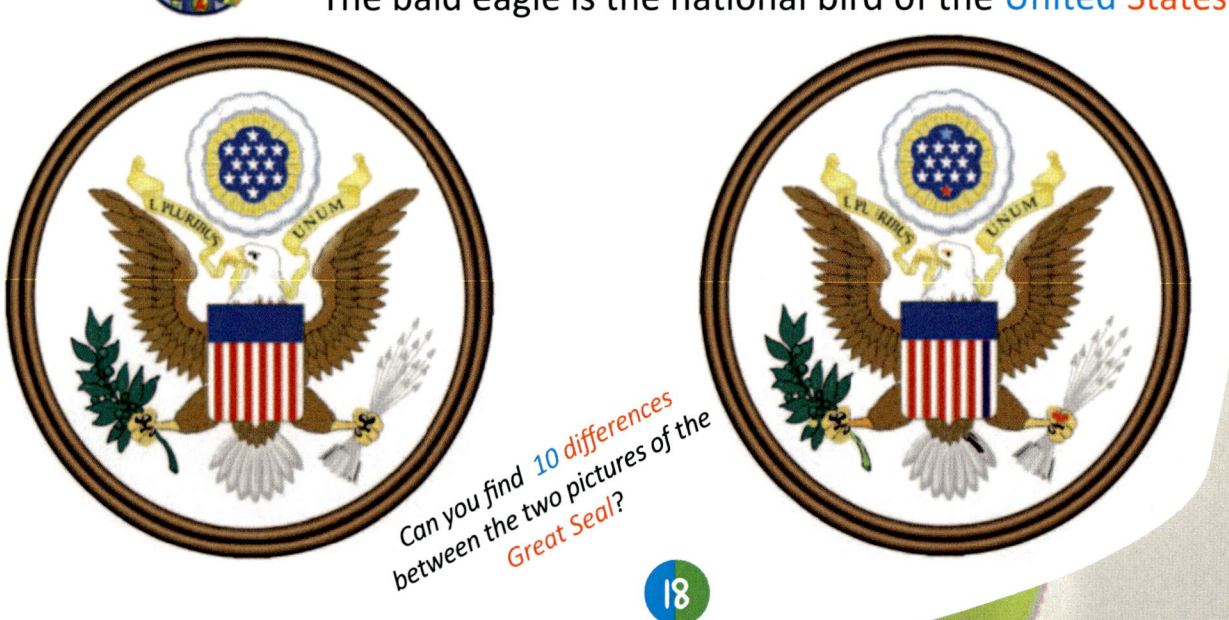

Can you find 10 differences between the two pictures of the Great Seal?

How can you buy things in the United States?

If you want to buy something in the United States, you have to have US dollars.
One dollar is equal to 100 pennies or 100 cents.

Did you know?

"Dollar" comes from a Czech word. Hundreds of years ago in the Czech Republic, silver from the mines was made into coins. They called the coins Joachimsthaler, or taler for short. That sounded like "dollar" in English, and the British people started calling any large silver foreign coin a dollar. The United States decided to use the word "dollar" as the name for its money in 1785. All European countries measure the worth of their money by comparing it to the value of the US dollar.

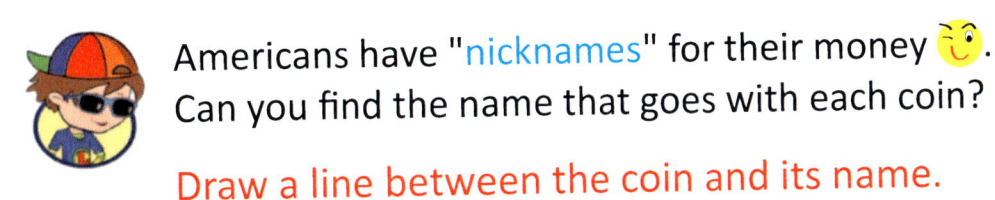

Americans have "nicknames" for their money 😜.
Can you find the name that goes with each coin?

Draw a line between the coin and its name.

A DIME equals 10 cents.

A QUARTER is 25 cents.

19

Why is 10 cents called a DIME?

"Dime" is an old French word that means "10th." A dime is 10 cents, or a 10th of a dollar.

Why is a dollar called a BUCK?

A "buck" is a male deer or moose. It is said that the American Indians used the skins of bucks—not coins—as money. So when the first Europeans came to America, they bought things from the Indians and sold them things using buckskins for money. One buckskin was equal to one dollar. Even when the US started using coins and bills for money, people still called dollars "bucks."

Try to find these words in the following word search puzzle:

- [ ] dollar
- [ ] Great Seal
- [ ] Washington
- [ ] dime
- [ ] capital
- [ ] buck
- [✓] Leonardo
- [ ] USA flag
- [ ] quarter

q	u	a	r	t	e	r	c	u	n
l	e	o	n	a	r	d	o	d	g
a	f	h	t	v	b	i	a	d	e
k	j	s	x	b	h	m	w	o	v
g	r	e	a	t	s	e	a	l	c
u	e	c	a	p	i	t	a	l	c
z	d	i	u	s	a	f	l	a	g
e	v	b	u	c	k	o	a	r	a
w	a	s	h	i	n	g	t	o	n

20

Once upon a time: some history ...

Did you ever hear of Christopher Columbus? Do you know who came to the Boston Tea Party? What is the Fourth of July? The US has a long, rich, and very interesting history!

Picture of Christopher Columbus

US history starts with Christopher Columbus, the man who discovered America. Well, the truth is he probably wasn't the first European to come to the shores of America 😜. But his visit in 1492 is the first time we have proof that a European set foot on American soil. In fact, Christopher Columbus was really trying to sail around the world to get to Asia on the other side 🙂.

And where did America get its name?

America is named after the Italian explorer Amerigo Vespucci.

Did you know?
Until the day he died, Christopher Columbus did not know that he came to America. He was sure he had landed on the coast of India 🙂.

Like Columbus, he was trying to sail around the world to get to Asia. But Amerigo Vespucci knew he had instead found a "New World" (different from Europe, or the "Old World"). In 1507, a German man was drawing the first world map that showed the New World. He decided to name it "America" after "Amerigo." He wrote the name on the map, and after that, everyone started calling it America.

After Columbus, the Spaniards came to America. They were the first Europeans to stay and live in America. French traders came next, and then the Dutch and English. Within 200 years, England had 13 colonies along the East Coast and had taken over most of the French and Spanish colonies.

Quizzes!

Do you remember how many stripes are on the American flag and why?
(You can go back to "Flags, Symbols, and Coins" if you need a reminder 😉.)

Did you know?

Some people didn't come to America by choice. Africans were brought to the US to be slaves 😟.

Why did people leave Europe and come to America?

They had many good reasons. Some were looking for religious freedom. In America no one told them what religion to follow. Other people wanted a chance to have lots of farmland so they could support their families better. Others thought they would find jewels and gold! And many came for the adventure. But they were all looking for new opportunity, a better life, and the freedom to live the way they wanted.

So how did 13 British colonies become a giant country like the USA???

In America, everything was new and different from Europe. When the first Europeans got here, the land was covered with a thick, deep forest. They had to chop down the trees so they could build cities and plant crops. As the colonies grew, the people developed their own customs, and they began to think of themselves as Americans instead of Europeans. But even though they lived in America, the people in the 13 colonies had to pay high taxes to the British government in Europe. That made them really, really mad 😳.

Have you ever been to a tea party?
Have you heard about the Boston Tea Party?

Well, it wasn't exactly a party—but some people wore costumes! It happened in 1773. Three British ships came to Boston Harbor filled with tea. (The early Americans really liked tea!) The British government said the colonists had to pay a tax before the tea could be unloaded from the ships. The colonists didn't think that was fair. So in the middle of the night, hundreds of them dressed up like Indians and went to the ships, and they dumped all the tea into the water!

This was called the Boston Tea Party. It's an important event in history because it started the Americans' fight for independence from the British, and it led to the Revolutionary War.

So what kind of tea party would you rather go to?

Don't worry, there's a happy ending.

Ten months later, the colonies formed their own Continental Congress. And what happened then? Nearly three years after the Boston Tea Party, on the historic day July 4, 1776, the 13 colonies signed the Declaration of Independence from the British government. Ever since, this day has been celebrated as Independence Day.

Signing of the Declaration of Independence

Quizzes!

So what is Independence Day called in the United States? _____

Did you know?

After the Declaration of Independence, Americans still had to fight the Revolutionary War to become free from British rule. The British didn't accept that the United States was an independent country until seven years later 😟.

And how do Americans celebrate their Independence Day?

It's a day of fun for everyone, with joyful parades, picnics, and big fireworks shows at night.

How do you celebrate Independence Day in your country? _____

Is it the same or different from how the United States celebrates? _____

Did you know?

In Leonardo's country, they celebrate Independence Day by playing trumpets and drums all night 😊.

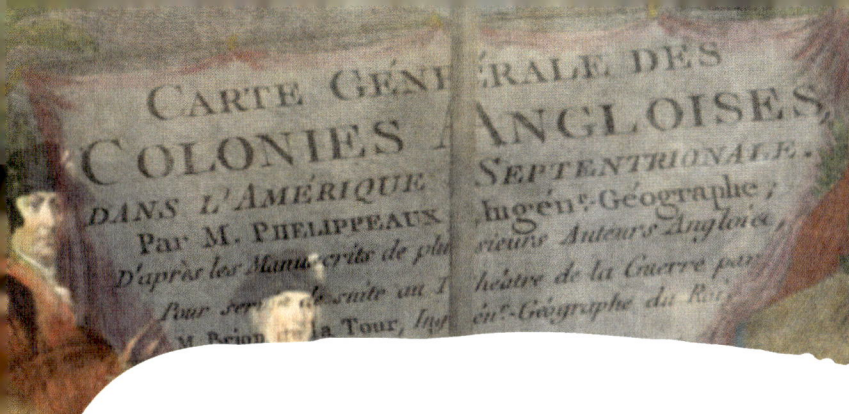

Go west, young man!

The United States began as a small country with 13 states—all located on the East Coast, bordering the Atlantic Ocean. But in 100 years, the US had grown to reach the Pacific Ocean on the West Coast! So how did that happen?

After winning the Revolutionary War, the US signed a peace treaty with Great Britain in 1783. That treaty gave the US a lot of the land Britain owned in America—making the United States twice as big!

Then 30 years later, the size of the country doubled again—after the US government bought a lot of land from France! (That was called the Louisiana Purchase.) The US fought wars with Mexico to get the land for Texas and other states in the Southwest—including California on the West Coast. The US bought some land from the native Indian tribes, but it also fought the Indians and took land they had lived on for many thousands of years.

On the trail west ...

Americans from the East (and new European immigrants) left their homes and moved west to settle the new wild land. They went for the same reasons that people came to America in the first place: they wanted more land, more opportunity, and more freedom.

Have you heard of the pioneers?

They traveled west in groups of covered wagons called wagon trains. The pioneers packed food and all the things they would need for their new life. In the wilderness, there were no stores to buy supplies.

The trip was hard and dangerous. Some people became sick and died on the way. The dirt trails got very muddy when it rained, and the wagons got stuck. The pioneers had to cross wild rivers and mountains. They had to fight unfriendly Indians, as well as bandits who wanted to steal their things.

Once they arrived, the pioneers cleared the land and planted crops. They chopped down trees to **build log cabins**. They even made their own soap and candles from ashes and animal fat.
(No electric lights back then!)

Did you know?

Children had the job of chasing deer and squirrels away from the fields. Otherwise, those animals would eat the crops, and the pioneers wouldn't have enough food!

Children were very important in pioneer life.

Girls helped with cooking, tending the garden, and making clothes. Boys worked with their fathers to build fences, plant crops in the fields, and chop the wood for fireplaces. Both boys and girls helped care for farm animals such as cows, horses, and chickens.

Leonardo wants to know whether you would have liked to be a pioneer! What would have been your favorite part?

About American culture and Americans

So far we've been talking about the United States and its history, but we haven't talked about the people who live there—the Americans 🙂.

What are they like? What do they like to do in their free time? What music do they like to listen to? What do they like to talk about?

Americans are very generous, polite, and kind. They work hard and follow the rules. They are patient when they have to stand in long lines at restaurants, shops, and events.

Americans are also very patriotic.* They fly their flag proudly in many places—at government offices, schools, homes, and stores. The national song, or anthem, is played at public events, and the Americans usually stand up, put their hands on their hearts, and take off their hats while it plays.

* Patriots are proud of their country, loyal to it, and willing to fight for it.

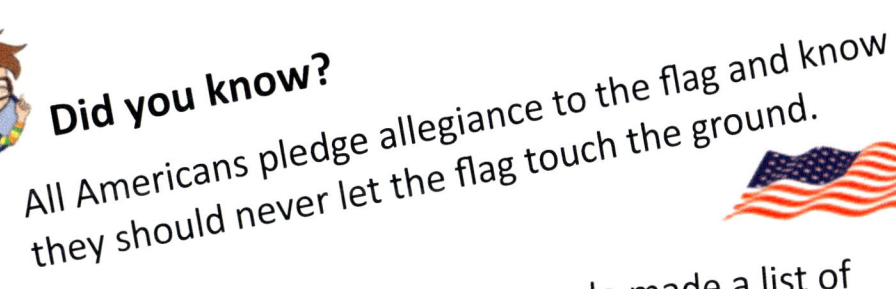

Did you know?

All Americans pledge allegiance to the flag and know they should never let the flag touch the ground.

Quizzes!

People have many nicknames for the USA. Leonardo made a list of these names, but he got a little mixed up. Help him figure out which nicknames are real and which ones are mistakes:

- ⭐ Uncle Sam
- ⭐ The New World
- ⭐ The land of choice
- ⭐ The Land of Opportunity
- ⭐ The States
- ⭐ The 50 states federation
- ⭐ Yankeeland
- ⭐ The Johnathan

Answers: Uncle Sam, The New World, The Land of Opportunity, The States, Yankeeland

What kind of music do Americans like to hear?

Soul music, jazz, pop, rock, country, hip-hop—even classical ... Anything goes! Americans love music, musicians, singers, bands, and orchestras.

Jazz was invented in America. It began during slavery when the African music of the slaves met European music—interesting meeting! Both sides combined their rhythms, and jazz was born. Jazz has some basic rules—and a lot of improvisation (making up the music as you play).

Soul music also comes from the US. How does soul music sound? Soul singers have deep and sometimes raspy voices. And a lot of times, a saxophone "sings" along with them.

Country music comes from folk songs and cowboy songs in the southern United States. You can recognize it by the string instruments—such as mandolins, banjos, fiddles, and guitars—along with harmonicas or accordions. Sometimes you can tell country singers by their cowboy clothes: cowboy hats, cowboy boots, and leather jackets.

Famous music stars in America

America has some of the world's biggest music stars of all time. (Some of them your parents know, and some of them you probably know.) Have you heard of Elvis Presley, Michael Jackson, Madonna, or Britney Spears?

What other American singers or bands do you know? _____

Who knows why it's called pop music?

Quizzes!

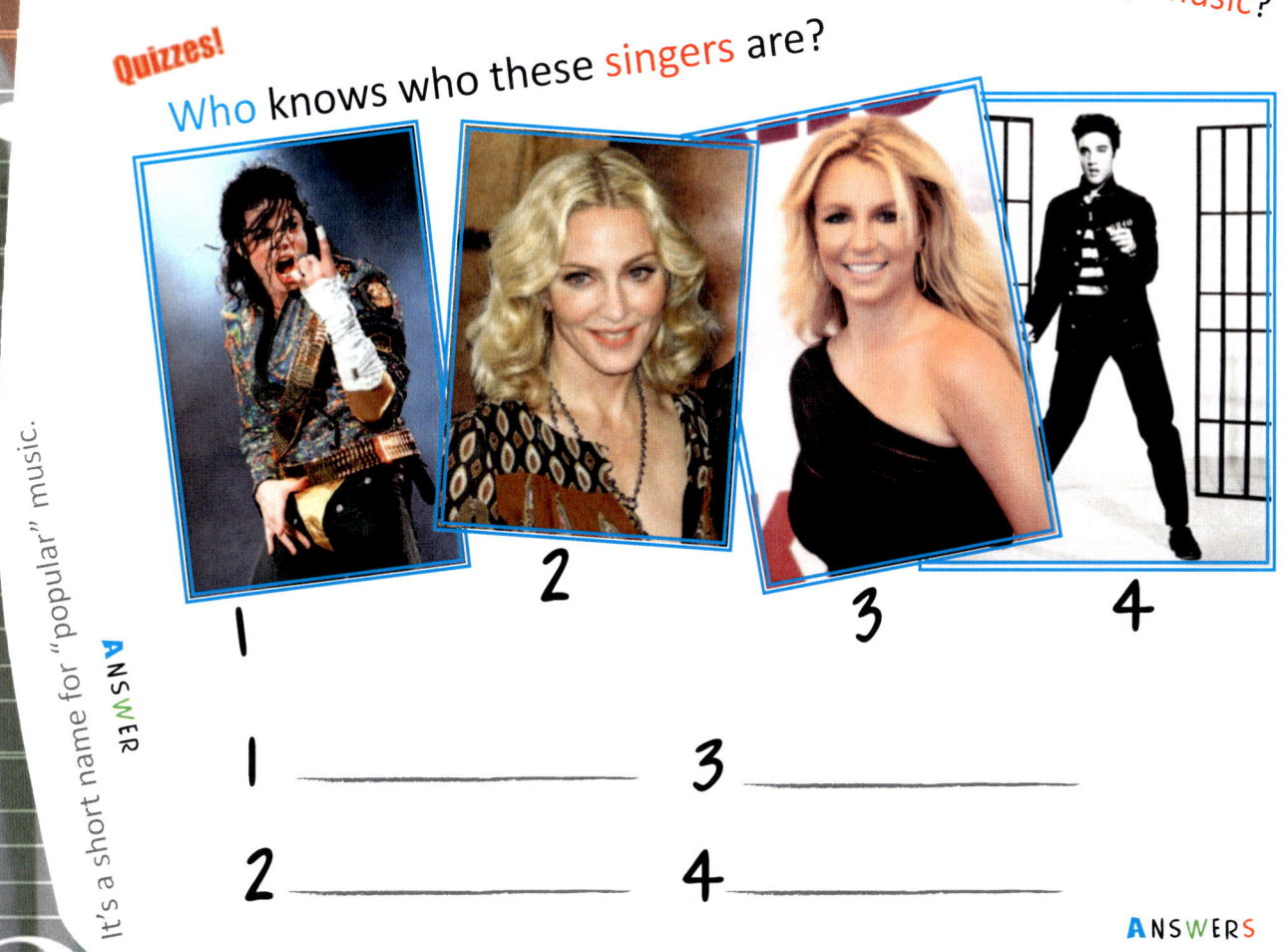

Who knows who these singers are?

1. _____   3. _____

2. _____   4. _____

ANSWER: It's a short name for "popular" music.

ANSWERS: 1 Michael Jackson, 2 Madonna, 3 Britney Spears, 4 Elvis Presley

29

The American MTV Video Music Awards are one of the most important events in the world of music. Everyone who works in the music industry and all their fans are eager to see who wins. But the Grammy Awards are the most important event in the US music scene and worldwide. The show is broadcast live throughout the world, and awards are given to musicians in 30 different music styles.

Hollywood and American films

Who knows where Hollywood is?

ANSWER: Los Angeles, California

How can we talk about America without talking about movie stars, movies, and … Hollywood!

America is the film capital of the world, and many, many movies are made in the US every year.

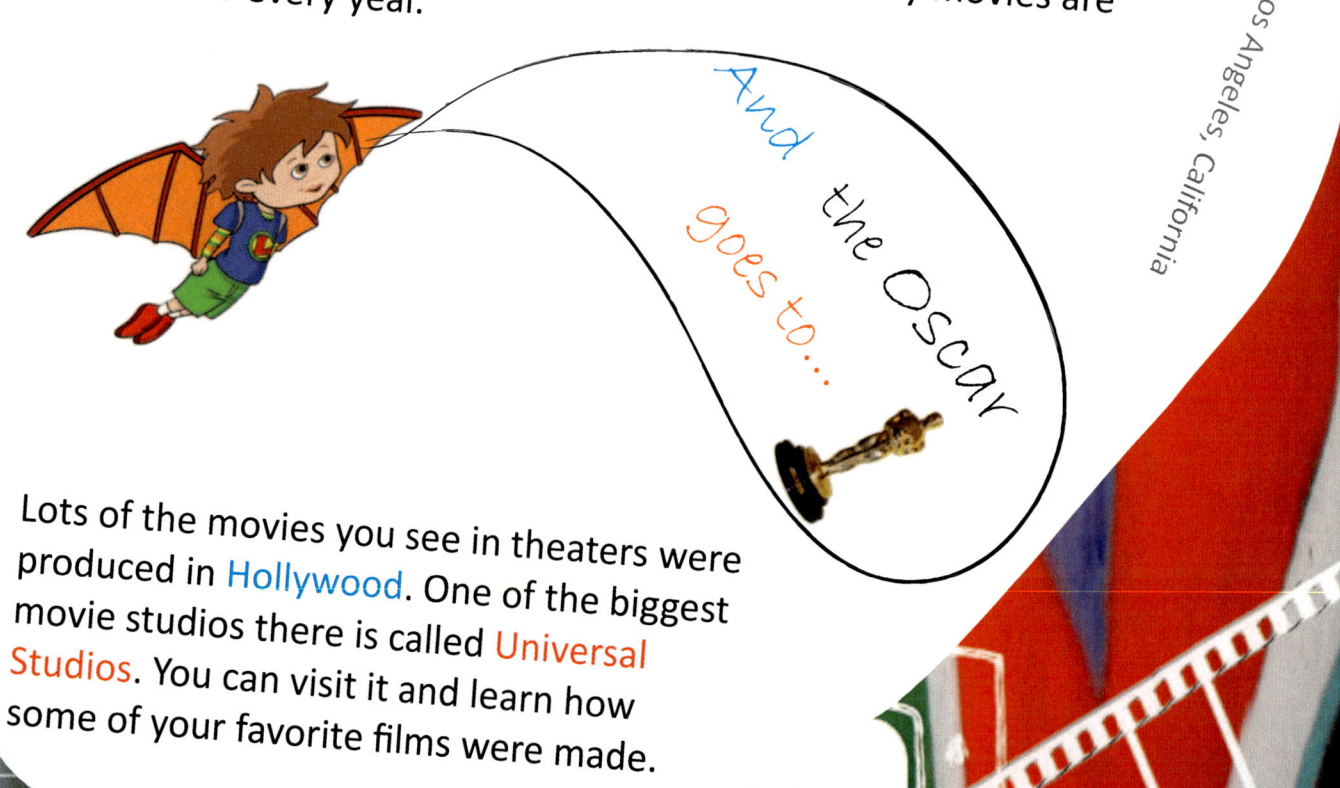

And the Oscar goes to…

Lots of the movies you see in theaters were produced in Hollywood. One of the biggest movie studios there is called Universal Studios. You can visit it and learn how some of your favorite films were made.

The Oscars, or Academy Awards, are the US awards for film. Winners get a small statue that is known by its nickname, "Oscar." Millions and millions of movie lovers in more than 200 countries watch this glamorous awards show on live TV. Awards are given in up to 25 categories, including best movie of the year and best foreign-language film.

Do you have a favorite American movie star? _____

What are your favorite movies? _____

Television

Americans watch more TV than any other country in the world. Many of the TV series that you and your parents know are American. Americans love TV shows of all kinds: action shows, romantic dramas, talk shows, soap operas, reality shows, comedies (called "sitcoms"—short for "situation comedies"), and more.

When did all this start?

The first television programs were shown in the US in 1928. And the first professional football game aired in 1939. Since then many successful TV series and sports games have been broadcast to the whole world.

The Emmy is the most important award in the world of TV. The cast and crew members of every TV show want to win **Emmy Awards**.

What programs or American TV series are your favorites?

1 _____   3 _____

2 _____   4 _____

Leonardo is a talented guy. He won all three prizes in America, but somehow he forgot what each prize was for and what it was called.

Can you help him figure it out?

1   2   3

1 _____   2 _____

3 _____

ANSWERS
1 Grammy (music)
2 Oscar (film)
3 Emmy (television)

Sports

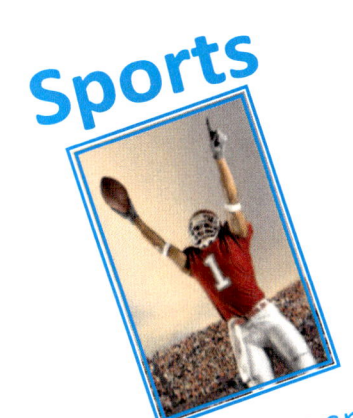

Have you heard of the *Los Angeles Lakers, New York Yankees,* or *Buffalo Bills* 🙂? The most popular sports in the United States are baseball, football, ice hockey, and basketball.

Do you know sports? Let's see! Connect the picture to the right sport:

basketball 1

baseball 2

ice hockey 3

football 4

Many American fans watch sports games in big stadiums or arenas—or at home on TV. They get together with their friends and cheer for their favorite team.

The championship game of the US National Football League is called the SUPER BOWL. This is the most popular sports event in the United States! Half of the country watches it on live TV—often at SUPER BOWL parties where people eat snacks and enjoy the game.

Baseball was invented in the US in 1845 from an English game called rounders. Baseball is called "AMERICA'S NATIONAL PASTIME." The championship is a series of games called the World Series, played every fall.

From left to right: 2, 4, 3, 1

ANSWERS

33

If you meet an American...

Just follow some basic rules—and you'll get along great!

Most of the time, you will call Americans by their first names. But if someone is introduced to you as Mr. Brown, be sure to call him Mr. Brown unless he tells you to use his first name 😉.

It is usually better not to talk to people you don't know, but if you need to talk to a police officer on the street, or a clerk in a store, or another adult you don't know, just call them "Sir" or "Ma'am."

Americans will often ask, "How are you?" A good way to answer is: "I'm fine, thank you, and how are you?" When you leave, you can say: "Have a nice day!"

Can you guess which one of these people is American?

Let's see! Connect each picture to the right country's traditional dress:

- British traditional dress
- Native American traditional dress
- French traditional dress

The first indoor shopping mall in the world was built in the US state of Minnesota in 1956. (They needed it because the winters are very long and very cold in Minnesota!) Today Minnesota has one of the most popular malls in the world—the Mall of America. If you spent just 10 minutes in every store, it would take you 86 hours.

How are you?
I'm fine, thank you, and how are you?
Have a nice day!

Making small talk with AMERICANS

Did you know?

What is "small talk"? It's a short and polite conversation that you have when you don't know someone very well, or when you don't have anything important to talk about. The weather or sports are always good subjects for small talk.

_____
_____
_____
_____

34

Let eat something — about American food

When you travel, you will often find new foods that are strange to you. But when you visit the United States, you may find a lot of foods you have heard of or even eaten before. America has it all! Who doesn't know hamburgers, pizza, macaroni and cheese, pancakes, and hot dogs?

Anyone hungry?

Where will you eat in the USA?

Americans love to eat at fast-food chains, family restaurants, cafeterias, and coffee shops.

How about playing a game with your family? Who can name the most fast-food restaurants?

And the winner is: _____

What's your favorite food? _____

What do you most look forward to eating in America?

_____

What will you eat in the USA?

BREAKFAST
DESSERT
LUNCH
DINNER

Remember when we told you that people from all over the world came to live in the US? Well, they all brought their favorite foods with them. That's why there are so many different kinds of food in the United States. Because you'll find foods from all around the world, it's hard to say exactly which foods are "American." But pizza, hamburgers, hot dogs, peanut butter, and ice cream sundaes have all become popular American food.

Have you heard the saying "As American as apple pie"?

What's for BREAKFAST

In America, you have to make a lot of room for breakfast. The menu usually includes these choices:

- A stack of pancakes with maple syrup
- A bowl of cereal with milk
- An omelet, or fried eggs with ham, sausage, or bacon
- Hash brown potatoes on the side
- Triangular-shaped toast
- Orange juice or grapefruit juice

What would you choose to eat?
Check and write your favorite dish. _____

Did you know?

More breakfast cereal is made in Battle Creek, Michigan, than in any other city in the world.

And what's for LUNCH?

Soups, salads, roast beef sandwiches, chicken sandwiches, peanut butter sandwiches, and hamburgers on buns with french fries or potato chips—these are all things Americans like to eat for lunch. Lunch is usually a smaller meal than dinner—or supper (both names are used for the evening meal).

Dinner at a restaurant usually starts out with an appetizer.*
After that comes soup or a small salad.

* What is an appetizer? It is a small plate of food you eat before your meal, while you're waiting for the rest of your food to be prepared.

The main course is called the entrée.
Steak, fish, chicken, and ribs with barbecue sauce are all popular foods at dinner. You may get a baked potato, a stack of french fries, or some mashed potatoes (whipped potatoes) with your meal 😊.

TRIVIA QUIZ: What do you know about the USA?

1. The United States is the _____ biggest country in the world.
   - A. Fifth
   - B. Second
   - C. Third
   - D. Most

2. Who was the first president of the United States?
   - A. George Washington
   - B. George Bush
   - C. Christopher Columbus
   - D. Indiana Jones

3. How many stars are on the US flag today?
   - A. 13
   - B. 50
   - C. 52
   - D. 40

4. Which of these is America's national bird?
   - A. Red hawk
   - B. Bald eagle
   - C. Bluebird
   - D. Blue Eagle

5. What country did Christopher Columbus think he was in when he discovered America?
   - A. India
   - B. Europe
   - C. Amerigo
   - D. Britain

6. What is "the Boston Tea Party?"
   - A. A big tea party celebrated by the Indians
   - B. A party celebrating the USA's Independence Day
   - C. Important event when the colonists got together and dumped tea in the harbor
   - D. A celebration for Christopher Columbus

7. When was the US Declaration of Independence from Britain signed?
   - A. July 4, 1776
   - B. July 14, 1776
   - C. When the Boston Tea Party was ended
   - D. July 4, 1556

8. If someone in the US gives you a buck, what do you have?
   - A. A 10-cent coin
   - B. A dollar
   - C. A gift
   - D. A greeting

9. Name one kind of music that started in America?
   - A. Jazz
   - B. Soul
   - C. Country music
   - D. All of the above

10. What is the name of the gold statuette Hollywood gives those who win awards for film?
    - A. Emmy award
    - B. MTV award
    - C. Oscar
    - D. Oliaster

11. What is American football's championship game called?
    - A. The Soup Bowl
    - B. The Big Series
    - C. The Super Game
    - D. The Super Bowl

ANSWERS

1-C, 2-A, 3-B, 4-B, 5-A, 6-C, 7-A, 8-B, 9-D, 10-C, 11-D

San Francisco
here we come!

Before you start reading about San Francisco ...

What do you already know about this city?

_____

_____

What are you most hoping to see and do in San Francisco?

_____

_____

Are you excited about the trip?

This is an excitement indicator. Ask your family members how excited they are (from "not at all" up to "very, very much"), and mark each of their answers on the indicator. Leonardo has already marked the level of his excitement ...

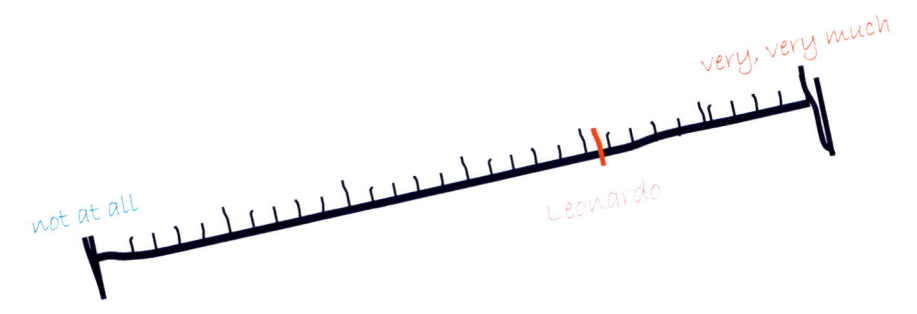

San Francisco, California: The City by the Bay

San Francisco is a big city in the big state of California! California sits on the West Coast of the United States of America. It borders the states of Oregon, Nevada, and Arizona, and the country of Mexico. But California's biggest border is its coastline that touches the Pacific Ocean.

Help Leonardo find California on the map of the United States.

Can you also help him find how many neighboring states California has? _____

ANSWER: Three states

Quizzes!

Which two states are bigger than California? Use the map as a clue!

ANSWER: Texas and Alaska are bigger.

In terms of size, California is only the third largest state. But it has more people than any other state in America!

40

The Golden State

Every state in the United States has a nickname. California's nickname is "The Golden State."

Can you think why California has this nickname? If you don't already know, you'll find the answer somewhere on this page …

Does **your** state or country have a nickname? What is it? _____

A few more things about California …
The Capital: Sacramento
What is the capital of **your** state or country? _____

State Motto: "Eureka!" meaning "I Have Found It!"
Do you know what they found? G _ _ _!
What is the motto of your state or country? _____

State Song: "I Love You, California"
What is the song of your state or country? _____

ANSWER: Gold

San Francisco, here we come!

San Francisco, the fourth largest city in California, is one of the most beautiful cities in the world! It is situated on a natural harbor called San Francisco Bay. The city is known for its steep hills, beautiful parks, different styles of architecture, historic cable cars, and excellent food!

Where did San Francisco get its name?

When the Spanish first came to California, they called this area Yerba Buena. That's Spanish for "Good Grass" or "Good Herbs." In 1848, the name was changed to San Francisco to honor Saint Francis.

What does San Francisco look like?

Here is a map of the city.
If you look closely, you can see that San Francisco is divided into different sections. These sections are called neighborhoods.

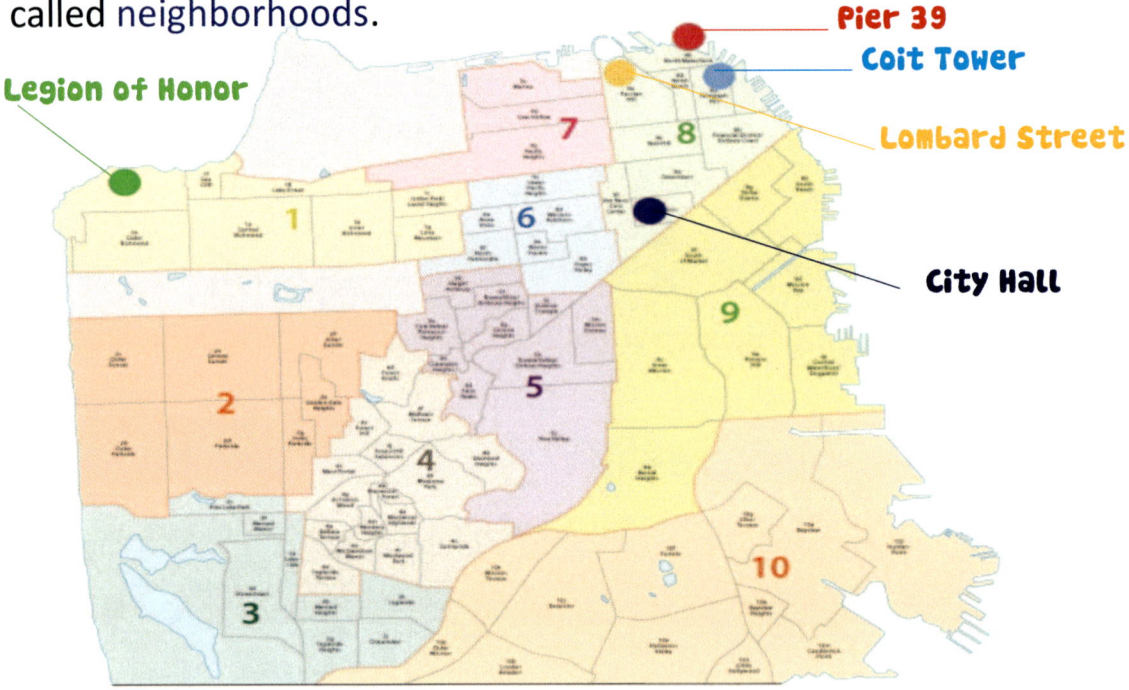

Legion of Honor
Pier 39
Coit Tower
Lombard Street
City Hall

Quizzes! In which neighborhood are these sites located?

Coit Tower _____
Pier 39 _____
Legion of Honor _____
Lombard Street _____
City Hall _____

In which neighborhood are you staying? _____
Mark it on the map.

Did you know?
San Francisco has many nicknames. It can also be known as "The City by the Bay," "The City That Waits," "Fog City," "Frisco," and just "The City."
Can you think of why San Francisco is called each of these different nicknames?

ANSWERS
Coit Tower-8, Pier 39-8, Legion of Honor-1, Lombard Street-8, City Hall-8

Gold Rush

San Francisco and the Gold Rush

Native Americans lived in the area that is now San Francisco for hundreds of years, but it did not become a real city until the Spanish arrived. When the city became San Francisco, only 469 people lived there! They included Ohlone Indians, Spanish Californians, Hawaiians, Europeans, South Americans, and New Zealanders.

San Francisco's population stayed small until 1849. That's when the Gold Rush started! James Marshall found gold at Sutter's Mill! When word got out, thousands of people rushed to California. They wanted to find gold, too, and "*strike it rich*!" These people were called forty-niners. Can you guess why? Though most of them were Americans, others came from China, Mexico, Europe, and Australia. The Gold Rush only lasted three years. Even when all the gold was gone, many forty-niners decided to stay in California.

Did you know?
Denim jeans were invented in San Francisco during the Gold Rush. Denim was first used as a thick material that was perfect for making tents to sleep in. But Levi Strauss noticed that the miners needed durable pants that would hold up while they worked. Denim pants (and Levi's) have been popular ever since!

Things you'll see only in San Francisco

Crooked streets, beautiful parks and gardens, cultural neighborhoods—there are plenty of attractions in San Francisco for you to see.

Now it's time for Leonardo to lend a hand! He has gathered information about the most popular sites and activities.

Sourdough bread. The yeast needed to make sourdough bread only grows in San Francisco—and the city has made this tasty bread famous! Try a sandwich on sourdough, or eat soup out of a bowl made of sourdough.

Have you noticed the many heart-shaped statues?

Every year, different artists paint or decorate big heart-shaped statues. Then they place the statues in different spots around the city. At the end of the year, the statues are auctioned off to raise money for charity! The statues are always in different places, so keep your eyes peeled! If you find a heart statue, take a picture of it.

Be sure to write down where you found it!

_____
_____

Getting around in San Francisco

There are several fun ways to travel around San Francisco.

One way to get around is by trolley.

The trolleys can take you just about anywhere in the city. They stop frequently and move slowly, so there are plenty of opportunities for you to take pictures of the things you see! San Francisco is one of the few cities left in the world that still uses old-fashioned trolley cars. The city brought old trolleys from all over the world to use here in San Francisco.

When you see a trolley, can you tell where it is from? Write it down!

You can also get around on San Francisco's metro system called MUNI (pronounced like "*myoo-nee*"). MUNI runs underneath San Francisco's streets. It can get you very close to many popular places, so you won't have to walk very far.

Can you think of one advantage and one disadvantage to using MUNI to sightsee?

Advantage _____

Disadvantage _____

Why is it called MUNI? MUNI is short for San Francisco MUNIcipal Railway. "Municipal" means it belongs to the city.

The famous cable cars!

The most famous way to travel in San Francisco is on a cable car! Cable cars are a good way to get from one end of the city to the other. They also make it much easier to get up those big hills! You will likely have to wait in a long line to ride on the cable car, but it's worth it!

Quizzes!

Can you guess how fast the cable car travels?

a. Nine miles per hour (14.5 km/hour)

b. Three miles per hour (4.8 km/hour)

c. Five miles per hour (8 km/hour)

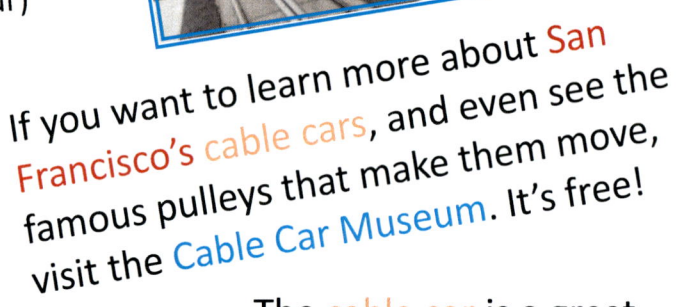

ANSWER: a. Nine miles per hour (14.5 km/hour)

If you want to learn more about San Francisco's cable cars, and even see the famous pulleys that make them move, visit the Cable Car Museum. It's free!

Tip!

Try to get a seat up front, and ask the cable car conductor to ring the bells!

The cable car is a great way to travel from Union Square to Fisherman's Wharf! Take the Powell-Hyde line for the most scenic route! **As you ride over the hills and through the streets, mark on the map what you see.**

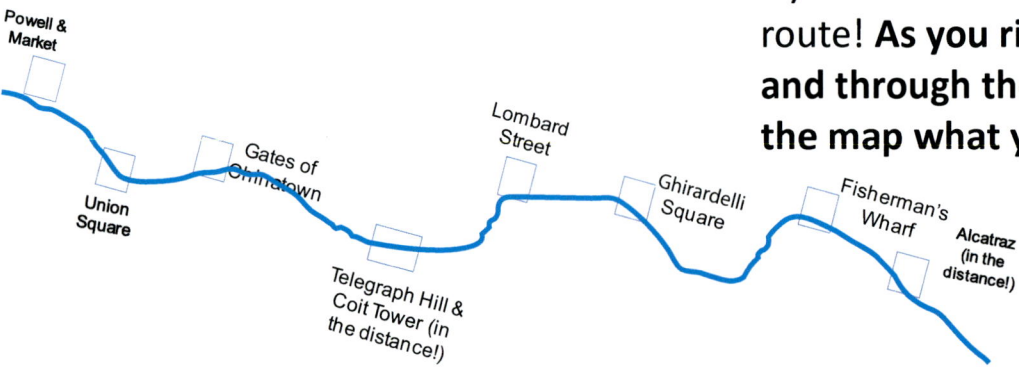

Powell & Market — Union Square — Gates of Chinatown — Telegraph Hill & Coit Tower (in the distance!) — Lombard Street — Ghirardelli Square — Fisherman's Wharf — Alcatraz (in the distance!)

46

The heart of San Francisco ...
Union Square

Union Square is the bustling heart of San Francisco!

Locals and tourists alike come to Union Square to go shopping. During the holidays, a big Christmas tree and a big menorah are lit up. An ice-skating rink is set up in the center of the square for people to enjoy.

Union Square wasn't always as luxurious as it is now. During the Gold Rush, it was called Morton Street. It was famous for its saloons and gambling halls. In fact, Morton Street was such a bad area that even the police were scared to go there.

Did you know?

San Francisco was nowhere near the fighting during the American Civil War between the Union and the Confederates. But Union Square got its name because it was once used for rallies to support the Union Army.

Stand in the middle of Union Square facing Macy's. What do you see?

On the left: _____
In front: _____
Behind you: _____
On the right: _____

ANSWERS

ON THE LEFT: Neiman-Marcus; IN FRONT OF YOU: Macy's windows and The Cheesecake Factory; BEHIND YOU: Saks Fifth Avenue; ON THE RIGHT: The Westin St. Francis Hotel

Union Square – a special place

Today, Union Square has many fancy restaurants and hotels. Stores like Louis Vuitton and Prada make it a world-famous spot for shopping! Many people who live in San Francisco come to Union Square for a special night on the town. They eat dinner at a nice restaurant, and then go to one of the many nearby theaters.

My impressions of Union Square: _____

Which is the most beautiful building? _____

Did we buy anything? If so, what? _____

How did we spend our time in Union Square? _____

_____

Tip!

For great views of San Francisco, go into the Westin St. Francis Hotel and ride the glass elevators. If you lean your head against the glass, you can see the whole city.

Chinatown ...

A Chinese neighborhood inside San Francisco

Visiting Chinatown is like taking a small jump into China. During the Gold Rush, many Chinese immigrants moved into this one section of the city. They wanted a place where they could continue their Chinese traditions and feel as if they were back home. Today, Chinatown feels a lot like it did during the Gold Rush! Of course, even tourists are invited to visit and enjoy. When you enter Chinatown, you'll notice new smells, tastes, music, and colors! Chinatown feels different than the rest of San Francisco.
Do you hear people speaking Chinese on the streets? Have you noticed all of the different street signs? They're written in Chinese!

Did you know?

Do you notice the interesting roofs on many of Chinatown's buildings? They look like they have several roofs sitting on top of each other. These buildings are called pagodas. It is believed that they keep spirits (ghosts) from climbing into the houses, because the spirits will trip on the curved edges of the roof.

Pass through the Dragon Gate and enter Chinatown. It's a must-see for visitors to San Francisco! It is the most popular place for tourists to visit in the whole city. It attracts more tourists than even the Golden Gate Bridge!

唐人街

Festivals in Chinatown

A PARTY IN CHINATOWN!
Chinatown is almost always busy, but it's especially busy during festival time. In January or February, San Francisco has a big street fair and parade to celebrate the Chinese New Year. Every autumn, they celebrate the Autumn Moon Festival. People eat lots of food, especially moon cakes—moon-shaped pastries with a sweet filling.

Tip!
Most tourists just stay on Grant Avenue, Chinatown's "main street," but it's worth it to explore some side streets.

Did you know?
The Fortune Cookie Factory in Ross Alley makes over 20,000 cookies per day!

Did you know?
Chinatown in San Francisco has the largest Chinese population in the world outside of Asia!

Leonardo wrote his name in Chinese. Can you write like him?

萊昂納多

Have you ever visited a cookie factory? Find Ross Alley and go to the Fortune Cookie Factory.

50

Things to do in Chinatown

Chinatown is a great place to learn about Chinese culture! Do you know what a Chinese lantern looks like?

Quizzes! Which one of the pictures is a Chinese lantern?

A   B   C

ANSWER: A

A few things to do in Chinatown—check off the things you do!

◯ Visit a Chinese restaurant or snack stand and try one new food you might enjoy. What did you try?

_____

◯ Count the dragons! How many dragons did you find?

_____

◯ Take a picture of a cricket in a cage.

◯ Greet a Chinese person by saying "Ni-hao!" ("Hello!" It's pronounced like Nee-how).

◯ Try a freshly baked fortune cookie.

◯ Pick up a souvenir. What did you get?

_____

51

The Golden Gate Bridge

The Golden Gate Bridge is one of the most famous images in the world.

A GOLDEN IDEA!

In the 1930s, San Franciscans wanted an easier way to connect the two sides of the San Francisco Bay.

For many years, San Franciscans tried to find a better way to get from the city of San Francisco to Marin—but engineers claimed a bridge would be impossible to build or too expensive.

Only one engineer, Joseph Strauss, believed there was a way to connect the two sides of the bay. Not only did he build a new kind of bridge, he did so at an affordable cost.

For four years, thousands of designers and construction workers worked to build this beautiful bridge. Finally, the Golden Gate Bridge opened to the public in May 1937. Since then, nearly 1.5 billion people have crossed it!

Quizzes!

How long is the Golden Gate Bridge?

a. 1 mile (1.6 km)

b. 1.7 miles (2.7 km)

c. 10 miles (16 km)

d. 2.5 miles (4 km)

ANSWER: b

Interesting facts about the Golden Gate Bridge

The Golden Gate Bridge is 1.7 miles long (1,970 meters). When it first opened, it was the longest suspension bridge in the world! But 30 years later, a longer bridge was built in New York.

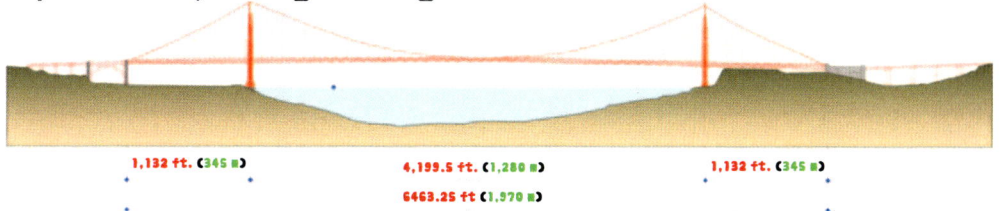

1,132 ft. (345 m)   4,199.5 ft. (1,280 m)   1,132 ft. (345 m)
6463.25 ft (1,970 m)

A few things not everyone knows about the Golden Gate Bridge:

- The bridge was supposed to be painted yellow with black stripes so that ships would be able to see it in fog. Luckily for us, not everyone thought this was a good idea. The official color of the bridge is not gold. The color is called "Golden Gate International Orange."

- The term Golden Gate refers to the Golden Gate Strait, which connects the bay to the Pacific Ocean.

- Eleven men died building the Golden Gate Bridge.

- When construction ended in May 1937, Chief Engineer Joseph B. Strauss wrote a poem titled "The Mighty Task Is Done." It is written somewhere on the Bridge.

- The bridge is especially designed to move! A swinging bridge might sound scary, but it actually means the bridge won't break when the earth shakes.

- A group of 50 employees and painters maintain the bridge.

- Each week, they use 1,057 gallons (or about 4,000 liters) of paint!

Tip! If there is time, you can walk or ride a bike all the way across the bridge!

Fisherman's Wharf and Pier 39

The city of San Francisco was built around the natural harbor of San Francisco Bay. The harbor is still a busy place! Ships and boats come and go from Pier 39, and tourists wander around the waterfront marketplaces at Fisherman's Wharf. It's easy to lose track of time here because there are so many things to see!

The nearby Aquarium of the Bay will give you a "diver's-eye" view of sea life in the San Francisco Bay. You can walk through clear tunnels to see fish, sharks, and other creatures.

The Venetian Carousel was carved and painted in Italy, but it's the only carousel in the US painted with images of its home city.

Can you guess how many people visit Fisherman's Wharf every year?

Quizzes!

a. 1 million
b. 1 billion
c. 15 million
d. 10 million

ANSWER: c

San Francisco is famous for its seafood and sourdough bread, both of which come from Fisherman's Wharf. What do you think of Fisherman's Wharf?

Smelly _____   Yummy _____   Crowded _____   Cool! _____

The sea lions of Pier 39

Usually, sea lions and other marine animals live on small islands just off San Francisco's coast. But after the big Loma Prieta earthquake of 1989, sea lions started hanging out at Pier 39. The city of San Francisco embraced the sea lions, and they are now a famous symbol of Pier 39!

Did you know?

The San Francisco Bay is not actually a bay. A bay is filled with ocean water. San Francisco Bay is really an estuary, which means it has a mix of fresh water and ocean water. It is the largest estuary on the West Coast of the United States.

As you may have noticed, sea lions are very talkative. They say exactly what is on their minds. Listen to the sea lions and try to make the ARK! ARK! ARK! sound that they are making. Do you sound like a sea lion? Maybe one of them will even answer you!

Why do seagulls fly over the sea?

Tip!

Love the sea lions? Pay a quick visit to the Sea Lion Center to learn more about them.

ANSWER: Because if they flew over the bay, they'd be bagels!

All things sea lion ...

Did you know?

There are more sea lions at Pier 39 in the winter than in the summer. During the summer months, the sea lions migrate south to the Channel Islands to breed.

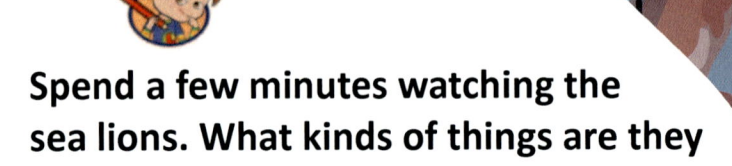

Spend a few minutes watching the sea lions. What kinds of things are they doing? How many are there?

_____
_____
_____

Fun facts about sea lions

- Sea lions are special mammals who can live in both the water and on land. The sea lions at Pier 39 sleep on their docks, but they'll go swimming when they want to eat.

- Do you see any sea lions swimming?

- A sea lion can swim up to 30 miles (48 kilometers) an hour! When they want to swim very fast, they glide on the surface of the water.

- A baby sea lion is called a pup.

- Are there any pups at Pier 39?

- Sea lions can live to be 30 years old. That's a long time for an ocean animal.

See the street performers!

When you're ready to leave the sea lions, walk back to the main street in front of Pier 39.

You are probably seeing a lot of street performers as you walk around Fisherman's Wharf and Pier 39! Many aspiring magicians, puppeteers, dancers, and even human statues(?) come here to test out their acts in front of tourists!

Write down all of the interesting street performers you see so that you will remember them. You can even take a picture of some of your favorites.

Funniest street performer: _____

Scariest street performer: _____

Strangest street performer: _____

My favorite street performer: _____

Exploring Alcatraz

Alcatraz has been a lighthouse island and a bird sanctuary, but it is most famous for being a prison! Until the mid-1900s, Alcatraz was a place for the most dangerous of all prisoners. Al Capone, George "Machine Gun" Kelly, and the "Birdman" all spent time in Alcatraz. Today, you can take a boat from Pier 39 to Alcatraz Island and take a tour of the prison!

Tip! Sometimes the weather on Alcatraz Island is colder or windier than in the city. Be sure to dress in layers and wear comfortable shoes.

Did you know?

When Alcatraz was a prison, there were many children who lived on the island. They lived there because their fathers were prison guards. Many of them had to take a boat to school every day. They had to follow many rules, like "No toy guns." Can you imagine living in a place like Alcatraz?

Taking the boat to Alcatraz is a great opportunity to view the beautiful San Francisco skyline. Can you see:

____ AT&T Park (baseball stadium) ____ Pier 39
____ The TransAmerica Building ____ Angel Island
____ Telegraph Hill & Coit Tower

Quizzes!

Help Leonardo count! How many bridges do you see? ____

ANSWER: Two bridges: The Golden Gate Bridge and the Bay Bridge

58

Prison life in Alcatraz

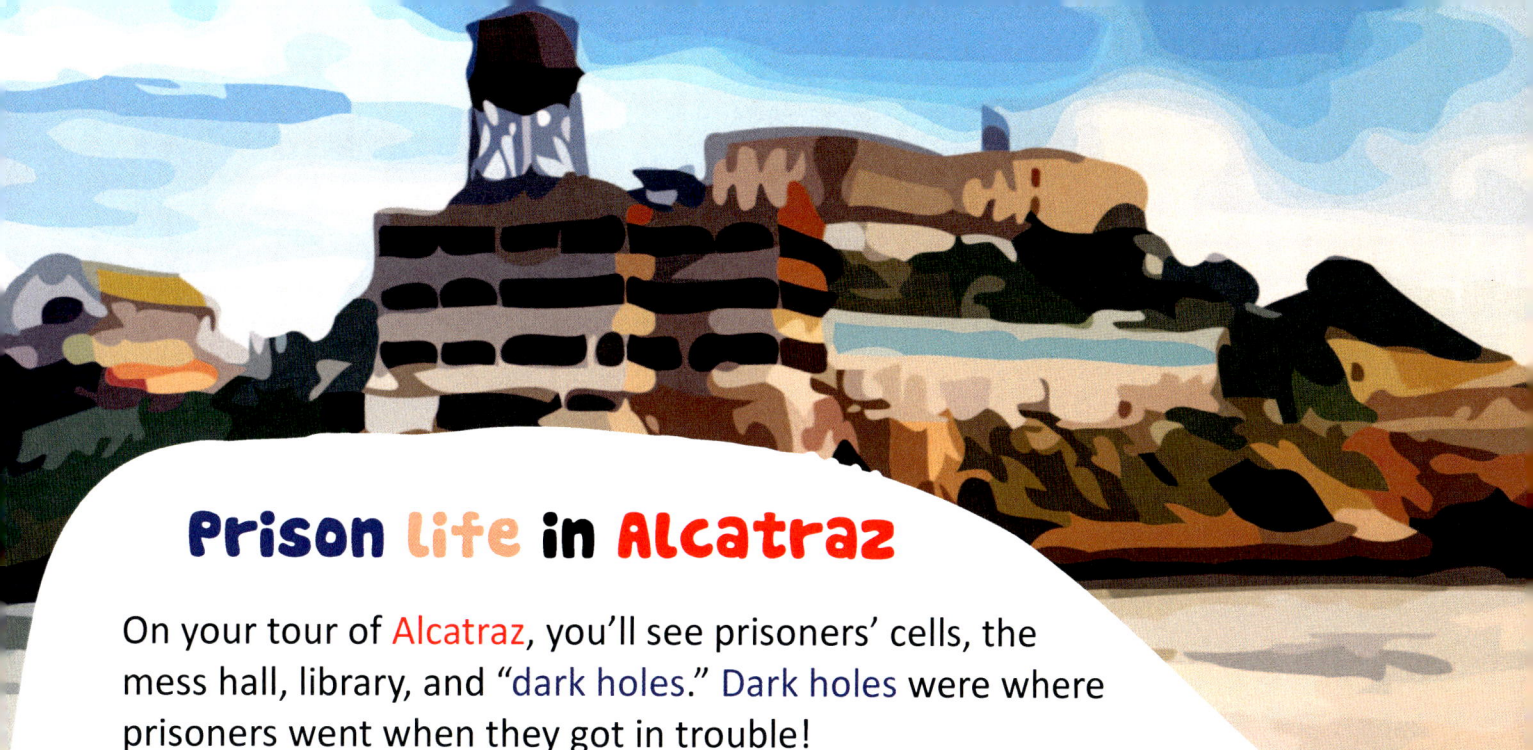

On your tour of Alcatraz, you'll see prisoners' cells, the mess hall, library, and "dark holes." Dark holes were where prisoners went when they got in trouble!

Find a cell and look inside. What do you see? Find eight items from the cell in the word search below:

Words you can find are:
blanket, toilet, mirror, shelf, matches, sink, comb, bed, ~~chess~~, paints

Which of these items would be most important to you?

```
B D S S S D T C
M G T I E E O R
O L N B K F I E
C K I N E X L S
N M A T C H E S
H L P H Q I T X
B R O R R I M R
S H E L F J X G
```

Did you know?

Alcatraz is named after a bunch of birds! Long before it was a prison, Juan de Ayala of Spain discovered the island in 1775. He named it Las Isla de Los Alcatraces, or "Pelican Island."

Quizzes! How many people successfully escaped from Alcatraz?

a. 30   b. 0   c. 1   d. 10

ANSWER: b. 0. About 60 people were caught trying to escape Alcatraz Island. Three people successfully made it off the island, but drowned trying to swim away.

North Beach - Little Italy

North Beach isn't actually a beach! It is a neighborhood famous for its Italian culture. That's why its nickname has become "Little Italy." In the early 1900s, many Italians made this neighborhood their home. During the 1906 earthquake, the Italians in Little Italy used barrels of red wine to put out the fire and save nearby Telegraph Hill!

Did you notice that the colors of the Italian flag are painted on each street lamp? Add the Italian colors onto the street lamp below!

What other Italian things do you see in North Beach?

_____

_____

Add the Italian decor

Did you know?
The same Grant Avenue you walked along in Chinatown is here in North Beach. This very long street is the oldest street in San Francisco. It is the heart of both Chinatown and Little Italy.

Telegraph Hill and Coit Tower

What does Coit Tower look like to you?
Does it look like a fire hose? Some people say Coit Tower was built as a monument to the firefighters who spent three days trying to put out fires after the 1906 earthquake. This is a nice story, but the tower's resemblance to a fire hose wasn't planned. The tower was built in 1931 with money left by Lillie Hitchcock Coit. She wanted her fortune to go to keeping San Francisco beautiful.

Inside the tower, you'll see murals painted by famous San Francisco artists. These murals show life during the Great Depression, when people were very poor. They can tell us a lot about how people lived then.

Coit Tower has some of the best views in San Francisco. Take the old-fashioned elevator to the top to see a 360-degree view of the city and the bay.
What sites do you see?

____ TransAmerica Building ____ Alcatraz ____ Golden Gate Bridge ____ Bay Bridge ____ Lombard Street ____ Pier 39

Did you know?
There are about 200 wild parrots who live on Telegraph Hill. It's not clear how they got there, but the cherry-headed conures and blue-crowned conures are now a famous part of San Francisco. See if you can spot some!

Golden Gate Park

Of all of the city parks in the United States, Golden Gate Park is one of the biggest! It's been around since the 1860s, when San Franciscans began to feel the need for a nice park like New Yorkers had in Central Park. Today, Golden Gate Park has museums, lakes, playgrounds, gardens, and much more! As you spend the day exploring the park, check off the things you see.

____ Dutch Windmill ____ Bison ____ The AIDS Memorial Grove

____ Horseshoe Pits ____ Japanese Tea Gardens

____ The Carousel ____ Botanical Gardens

We had lunch at _____

Museums we visited: _____

My favorite site(s) in the park: _____
_____

Did you know?
Golden Gate Park was once a big, free-range zoo! Today, the only animals left are the herds of bison in the Buffalo Paddock.

Tip! Rent a rowboat and paddle along the big lake in the middle of the park. Strawberry Island is fun to play on and a great place for a picnic!

The Japanese Tea Gardens

The Japanese Tea Gardens have been around since the California Mid-Winter Exposition in 1894. A few years after the Exposition, master gardener Makoto Hagiwara made the gardens even bigger and more impressive! This is now a beautiful, quiet oasis in the middle of the big city.

To fully experience the Japanese Tea Gardens:

_____ Cross over a traditional drum bridge.

_____ Try a warm cup of Japanese tea.

_____ Enjoy a fortune cookie.

_____ Find the bronze Buddha statue.

_____ Choose a hill and climb it to explore.

_____ Feed the koi fish in the koi ponds.

Tip! Find the bronze Buddha statue. Sitting among all of the plants and flowers is a bronze statue that is 10 1/2 feet (3.2 meters) tall. This Buddha was made almost 200 years ago! The actual name of this statue is *Amazarashi-No-Hotoke*, which means "Buddha who sits through sunny and rainy weather without shelter." Can you think of why the statue has this long name?

Did you know?

Makoto Hagiwara, the master gardener who made the Tea Gardens so beautiful, is also credited with inventing the fortune cookie!

Lombard Street

San Francisco has 43 hills, but Lombard Street is easily the most famous!

Lombard Street is often called the "crookedest" and the "steepest" street in the city, but actually it isn't. Vermont Avenue is the crookedest, and Filbert Street is the steepest.

Quizzes!

At which cross street do Lombard Street's curves begin? _____

At which cross street do they end? _____

ANSWER Begin: Hyde Street End: Leavenworth Street

ANSWER Eight

Hundreds of cars line up every day to drive down Lombard Street and experience the hairpin turns for themselves.

Did you know?

Lombard Street has appeared in many famous movies, television shows, and even video games. The most famous movie it's in is the classic film "*Vertigo*," by Alfred Hitchcock.

Did your family drive down Lombard Street? *How many turns did you count*? _____

Summary of the trip

How long did we stay in San Francisco? _____

At which hotel did we stay? _____

What kinds of transportation did we use? _____

Which sites did we visit? _____
_____
_____

The souvenirs I bought in San Francisco are: _____

The best food I ate in San Francisco was: _____

Record each family member's favorite site:

_____ : _____
_____ : _____
_____ : _____
_____ : _____

Grade the most beautiful places and the best experiences of the journey as a family.

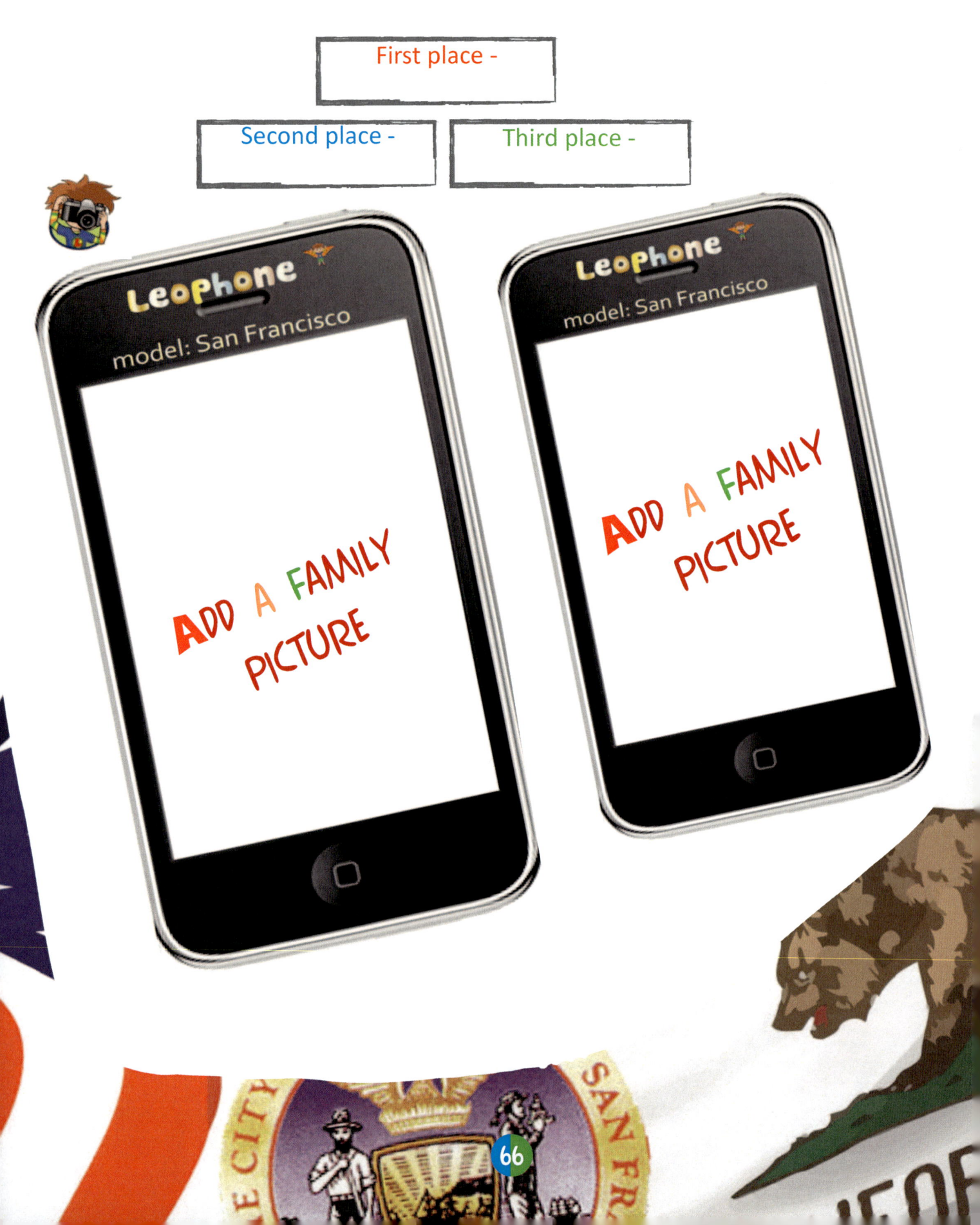

First place -

Second place -

Third place -

Leophone
model: San Francisco
ADD A FAMILY PICTURE

Leophone
model: San Francisco
ADD A FAMILY PICTURE

Quizzes

Use the hints to guess what these famous things found in San Francisco are.

1. If you take my elevator up 16 stories, you can see the entire city of San Francisco! If you walk through my lobby, you will get a glimpse of San Francisco's past.

   What am I? _____

2. We love to summer in San Francisco because it is nice and warm. We lounge around Pier 39, and only get up to go swimming and eat. Sometimes we are very loud, but the thousands of people who come to visit us do not seem to mind!

   Who are we? _____

3. Today, I am known for expensive shopping and fancy restaurants. But during the Gold Rush, people came to me to drink and gamble, and even policemen were scared to visit me. I am much happier today!

   What am I? _____

Answers

1- Coit Tower, 2- The sea lions, 3- Union Square

San Francisco Trivia!

1. Which famous article of clothing was invented in San Francisco?
   a. Dresses b. Galoshes c. Denim jeans d. Toe socks

2. San Francisco is famous for this kind of bread:
   a. Sourdough b. Wheat c. Rye d. Pumpkin

3. What is the oldest street in all of San Francisco?
   a. Grant Avenue b. Sutter Street c. Lombard Street d. 22nd Street

Answers

1-c, 2-a, 3-a

A San Francisco crossword

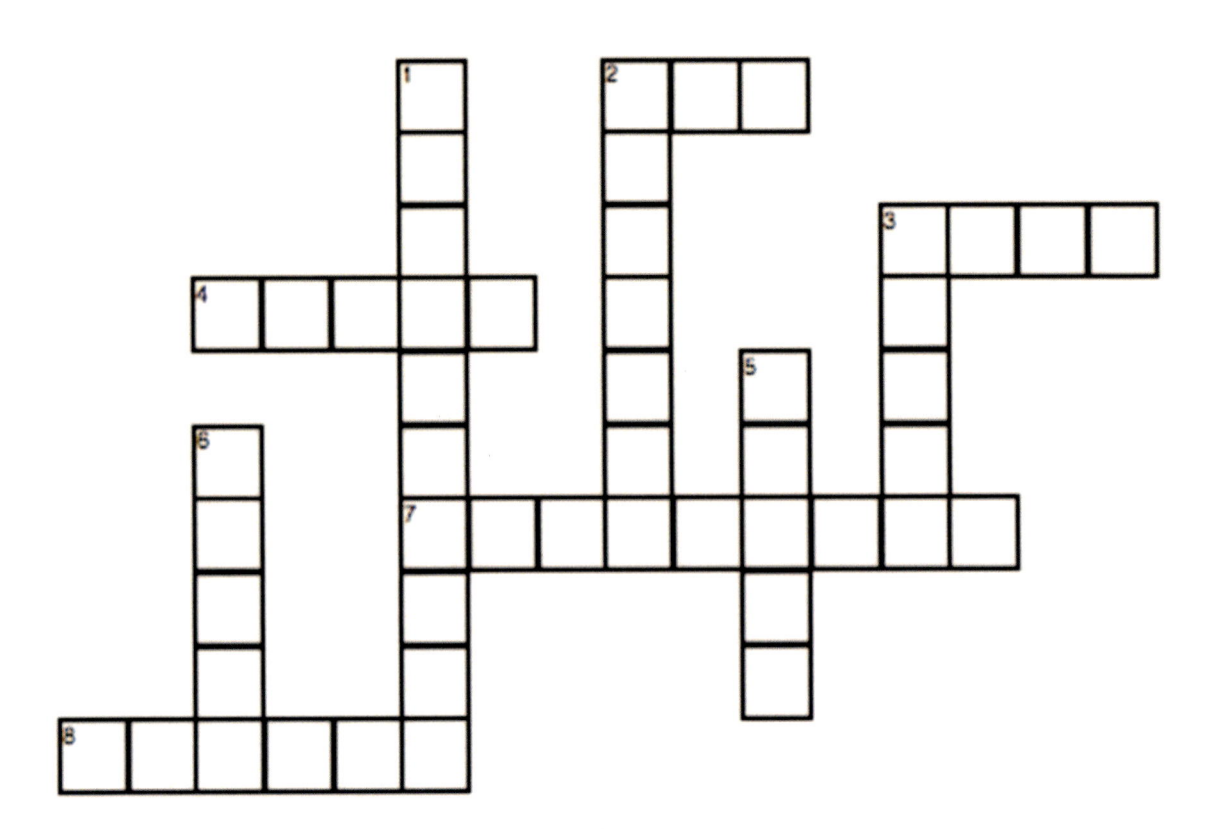

Across

2. A baby sea lion
3. _____ Tower
4. The famous jeans Levi Strauss invented
7. Where you'll find the Fortune Cookie Factory
8. Statue in the Japanese Tea Garden

Down

1. The state in which you'll find San Francisco
2. Telegraph Hill's tree-dwellers
3. _____ cars
5. San Francisco has 43
6. Sourdough is a type of _____

Can you break the code?

Use the key below to decipher Leonardo's journal entry about his trip to San Francisco

Q = A   **Z = O**   **M = E**   **J = I**

I had a great time in **SQN FRQNCJSCZ** (_ _ _ _ _ _ _ _ _ _ _)! I ate lots of Ghirardelli chocolate and **SZURDZUGH** (_ _ _ _ _ _ _ _ _) bread. I rode the **CQBLM CQR** (_ _ _ _ _ _ _ _) and even got to ring the bell as we passed Lombard Street. At Fisherman's Wharf, we saw lots of street performers, and I got to ride the **CQRZUSML** (_ _ _ _ _ _ _ _).

My favorite thing in San Francisco was Pier 39 and the **SMQ LJZNS** (_ _ _ _ _ _ _ _). Then again, I also loved the **PQRRZTS** (_ _ _ _ _ _ _) on Telegraph Hill and the shopping in **UNJZN SqUQRM** (_ _ _ _ _ _ _ _ _ _ _) and Chinatown. I guess I loved **MVMRYTHJNG** (_ _ _ _ _ _ _ _ _ _) about the beautiful City by the Bay!

Unscramble the Famous San Francisco Sites

Gldone eaGt rkaP _____

ireP 93 _____

ioBsn docadkP _____

nonUi qeuSar _____

aaztclrA _____

sFrnaihme's aWfrh _____

dmraLob eStrte _____

A journal

Date | **What did we do?**

A journal

Date	What did we do?

A journal

Date	What did we do?

Acknowledgment: All images are Shutterstock or public domain, except those mentioned below.
Attribution: 28ml-By Casta03 (Own work) [CC BY-SA 4.0 (http://creativecommons.org/licenses/by-sa/4.0)], via Wikimedia Commons; 28mcl-By David Shankbone (David Shankbone) [GFDL (http://www.gnu.org/copyleft/fdl.html) or CC-BY-SA-3.0 (http://creativecommons.org/licenses/by-sa/3.0/)], via Wikimedia Commons; 28mcr-By Glenn Francis Uploaded by MyCanon (Britney Spears) [GFDL (http://www.gnu.org/copyleft/fdl.html) or CC BY-SA 4.0-3.0-2.5-2.0-1.0 (http://creativecommons.org/licenses/by-sa/4.0-3.0 ...)], via Wikimedia Commons; 29ml-By Dave Gomez [CC BY-SA 4.0 (http://creativecommons.org/licenses/by-sa/4.0)], via Wikimedia Commons; 52mt-By Roulex 45 (Own work) [CC BY-SA 3.0 (http://creativecommons.org/licenses/by-sa/3.0) or GFDL (http://www.gnu.org/copyleft/fdl.html)], via Wikimedia Commons; 59mc-By Ian Chen (Own work) [CC BY-ND 2.0 (https://creativecommons.org/licenses/by-nd/2.0/) via Flicker.

Key: t=top;
b=bottom;
l=left;
r=right;
c=center;
m=main image;
bg=background

Made in United States
Orlando, FL
06 July 2025